WINTER ON SCILLY

This is Sue Lewington's second book
of sketches on the Isles of Scilly.
She has also published 'Sketches of
St. Ives' & 'Sketches around the Fal'.

Published by Dyllansow Truran,
Croft Prince, Mount Hawke, Truro,
Cornwall   TR48EE.

Printed by R. Booth at the
Troutbeck Press, Antron Hill,
Mabe, Penryn, Cornwall TR109HH

ISBN   1 85022 131 6 (cased)
ISBN   1 85022 132 4 (paperback)

Straw white

Scilly White &
Scilly pearl Hkink

Sol d'or

Raining again.

3

Old Quay, St. Martins - a westerly gale
The waves explode as they hit the end of the quay
& look as if they'll carry it all away. ..... And high tide at
Higher Town Quay

4   The sea sweeping up the quay, & the wall disappearing

South westerly gale – enormous squalls coming from behind cruthers & blotting out the view in a mist of blown rain & spray

sea & sky the same colours

grey green sea getting darker

The launch & post boat cancelled . .

5

A sure sign of winter –
the swallows have all gone, & the boats
have been pulled up. All those are in the
corner of the cricket pitch on Pool Green.
when the pool floods in a wet winter it reaches
to about this point & floods the entire pitch.
   Steve tells a wonderful story of chasing a cow half way round the
island to eventually catch it in the middle of the pool – both of
them exhausted. One pull on the tether & the cow falls over
& steve – who for the last hour has wished he could kill the cow
has to kneel in the water holding her head up so she doesn't
drown until someone sees him & helps to stand her up!

All the fishing ... are all very busy ready to be stored for the winter.

8

On a good day Keith can still get out & do
some fishing, but soon the punt
will be pulled up into the grass & stay
there until the spring...

unless we get
one of those
still, midwinter
days in
between the gales &
then he'll be out among
the Eastern Isles
fishing & 'wrecking'!

9

- Always a communal job - seems to me it consists of hours of discussion then minutes of frantic activity - then back to the discussion — The men would tell a different story i'm sure . . . .

NEMO

10

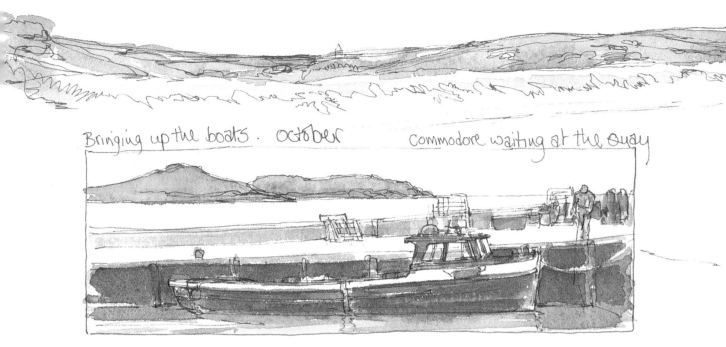

Bringing up the boats. october   Commodore waiting at the quay

MORVOREN

11

loading boats is always a communal affair. The men have 'making a chain' down to a fine art.

Everyone helps & you don't leave the quay till all arriving parcels are sorted. Someone will deliver unexpected ones.

Huge parcels arrive mysteriously in the kitchen, tiny packages with 'Tom, St Martins' on them are put carefully somewhere safe......

12 loading the mail — mostly boxes of flowers by post ...

A rough morning

It doesn't matter how bad the weather is - if the boat comes the shoppers are ready to go.

Trying to tie up the boat alongside the quay; Terry is the figure, soon to be up to his knees in white water, who's ready to let go the rope quickly if necessary.

passing migrants

Twitchers . . . . . or are they bird watchers . . .
we've just arrived on St. Marys on the Seahorse to get
our shopping & now Frazer's in deep discussion about
the possibility of getting to St. Agnes to see the American Robin
or the Great Grey Shrike . . . or perhaps some kind of warbler . . .

14

rough trip - wedged in
cabin I can enjoy the
view. All sky one second, then
sea . . . . . Rolling well!

Taking the mail to St. Agnes

The quickest way home after a trip
to the mainland - A ride on the
Mail boat to St Agnes & then St MARTINS.

SELECTED
ICEBERG LETTUCE

grilled

Laden down with
groceries & food
for Liv. fresh veg
boxes & bags

Blowing quite hard @
choppy sea

Home - with
the shopping
piled high...

16

A modern, covered boat for shopping trips now.
We're dry & comfortable & ... it's not nearly so EXCITING.

kirsty fast asleep

Boo Bog
Goddard
ST. MARTINS

Books

lots of identical
arrier bags - they take
ome sorting out on the quay

magnolia

coming home with the shopping - slowly - as it's a very low tide

SHARP WARF
WAITING ROOM

Red

Lin's cat
(been to the vet)

17

The sun going down over Samson
4pm ish — very cold, northerly
wind

A walk to White Island on the shortest day, dull, grey & cold.

Freds palm tree on White Island. He says he felt he was being watched. And twice saw a strange figure. I looked but didn't see anything. Though there was a strange atmosphere.

18

has rained & rained &
...ained January, & the...
...eeu now looks like a boating lake · Afternoon sun, long shadows

...oats, pulled up for the winter, nearly afloat again...

19

christmas groceries arriving.
Rain, wind, high tide, sea breaking
over the back of the quay.

It always seems to rain & blow harder
when the launch arrives...

groceries, parcels
booze, flower boxes -
All getting wet (& me.

High Tech...
r au oily rag

Filling the oil tank!
ce a week the launch
au 'oil day' r sometime
y remember to bring the oil..

21

CHRISTMAS on St. Martin's

Matthieu running up & down
all the time, Kenny playing the organ
& hard to see in this light!

The candle lit carol service
Caroline, Celia, The Bear, Margaret
& Christopher read the lessons &
Jackie a poem.

end wall lit
by an ochry yellow
light. strong soft

23

Going shopping - low tide. The gales have blown tons of sand
high up the beach & over the quay & hotel
garden. It looks just like drifting snow...

SNOW ~
- doesn't happen
very often -
maybe once in
the last Ten
years - & it only
lasted a day
or so.
So everyone had
to make the most
of it . . . . .

Text within the illustration:

PLEASE REMOVE FROM QUAY 4 SEPT 2011

ST. MARY'S BO...
PLEASE NOTE

TRESCO
BRYHER
SAMSON
ST AGNES
ST MARTIN'S
THREE ISLANDS

The end of the season on St Marys. By the end of October, there will be no tripper boats — the only visitors will be hitching lifts on the post boat, the launch, shopping boat & Sunday church boat. By Christmas we are quite used to this & when the bad weather stops the freight boat from coming from Penzance between Christmas Eve & The New Year we are all philosophical about the lack of fresh vegetables & empty shelves in the Co-op. The main crisis was the total lack of lemons in Hugh Town on Christmas Eve — what about my gin & tonic?

26

one shopping day with weather just like this, we waited in the shed,
rushed down to the boat as it arrived only to see a great wall of water
coming over the back of the quay. We all ducked & waited - got soaked

waiting for the launch.
A squall going over

from head to foot & looked up to see the boat leaving as it was
too rough to tie up! So it was home for coffee & no shopping ...

A DAY BORROWED from the gloom & cold,
wind & rain of winter,
It is WARM & still. birds singing, the tide coming in
☰ in gentle ripples
mounds of shells on the sand
& I have my favourite place entirely to myself...

But- I just realised that the end of the quay has changed shape
& sure enough there are two large rocks on the sand - I've
drawn it so many times & now it will never be the same again
I know Keith will be as concerned as me (it makes me want to
cry!) so I'll tell him. If it isnt mended the sea will work
away att it until its gone . . . . . .

28

29

LONG WINTER EVENINGS...

Alison
Andrew
Julia

Winter must be here! its the Reading Room
Reading Room meetings are seasonal # G.M - none of us have
time in the summer.-
So its back to hard chairs, cold room
r democracy - otherwise known as
arguments! (discussions)

All sorts of things go
on in here...
Table tennis, short mat bowls
line dancing (short lines!) country dancing, yoga, whist drive
keep fit, some kind of martial art with a strange name
r any party too big for a house! ... ...

Melodians, penny whistle,
Bodhran
Sea shanties & poems
plenty of wine & good Conversation.

31

DEREK'S PACKING SHED

Light & warm & full of sols &
whites. Julia, Celia, Jimmy & Cuth
tying. The flowers keep almost everyo
busy from the first whites
& sols in November throug
almost to Easter with the
last of the Daffs . . . .

Ken & Henry packing in the glasshouse
32   at Middletown

33

Fields of yellow — a lovely sight but it means that prices are so low
they're not worth picking. The golden yellow of the daffodils mix
with the acid, lemon yellow of the Bermuda buttercups as
soon as the sun comes out.

34

Papermaking at Middletown Gallery

There are 'sol'dors' everywhere in January. Maudy uses those not good enough to send to Market to make paper.

using petals & fibres from waste sols

A bowl of bright scented petals

35

with its home-made
wooden cab.
It looks like a cosy
garden shed on
wheels

Derek - waiting for a boat.

ing is coming....

. signs are it
coming of the
wdrops or the
ping of the birds-
the hammering r
oing, the tractors
orking r everyone
ladders,
iting, repairing
building.
ing ready for
he season...

37

A day out - a lift on the post boat from Lower Town to Carn Near on Tresco.

Tresco is only a 5min boat trip away & I haven't been here for over a year.

picnic on Tresco. February – a cold wind,
+ warm in the sun under the dunes.
pty beaches, home made bread &
mes & cream . . . & good company . .

picking sols in Barn Field
on a cold + muddy day.

40

Steve bringing home one bunch
from the old Quay Fields on a
Sunday afternoon.

the flower picking, packing r sending goes on r on . . . r on

41

pinks, anemones & daffodils.

42 Spring fields.   March.

Henry's cabbages... in the field behind the Reading Room... and protected, hopefully from rabbits. 43

one of the biggest spring tides of the year. I walked on sand way beyond Gutters,
& a line of breaking waves — & seagulls standing only up to their knees in
water showed where the sand bar stretched on towards Tresco.
But the tide had turned & it takes quite a while to walk back when I have to
stop to pick up shells & driftwood & just stand & stare . . . .

... And the other way to St. Helens & Tean.

45

pleasure boats, fishing boats
& Alfie's beautiful 'Pettifox'
all on Town Beach for their
spring clean. The moorings were
all checked on the big spring
tides last week. The Scillonian
starts sailing next week.
summer's nearly here . . . . .

46

47

SC 4

Keith's punts are back at Old Quay.
His nets & pots are being mended..
The moorings checked. The quay
comes alive once Keith's working again..
48